HENRY PURCELL IN JAPAN

POEMS BY

Mary Jo Salter

THE KNOPF POETRY SERIES

HENRY PURCELL IN JAPAN

Henry Purcell
in Japan

P O E M S   B Y

Mary Jo Salter

ALFRED A. KNOPF   NEW YORK   1985

THIS IS A BORZOI BOOK
PUBLISHED BY ALFRED A. KNOPF, INC.

Library of Congress Cataloging in Publication Data

Salter, Mary Jo.   Henry Purcell in Japan.

(Knopf poetry series ; 15)   I. Title.
PS3569.A46224H4   1985   811'.54   84-47849
ISBN 0-394-53657-6
ISBN 0-394-72762-0 (pbk.)

Manufactured in the United States of America

FIRST EDITION

ACKNOWLEDGMENTS

The following poems (sometimes in slightly different form) appeared in these magazines:

The Atlantic Monthly: "England"; "Love Poem for a Poet"; "At City Hall"; "Welcome to Hiroshima"

Grand Street: "On Reading a Writer's Letters"; "Shisendō"

Heatherstone Review: "The Season of Metaphor"

Kenyon Press: "Refrain"

The Nation: "'Officer and Laughing Girl'"; "On Removing Summer from the Public Gardens"; "Anthropod"; "Luminary"; "At the Public Baths"; "Amphitheater with Trees"

New England Review: "For an Italian Cousin"; "Facsimile of a Chapel"

The New Republic: "Two Pigeons"; "Rocky Harbour, Newfoundland"; "Among the *Ningyō*"

The New Yorker: "Henry Purcell in Japan"; "Expectancy"

Poetry: "Japanese Characters"

Yale Review: "Mary Cazzato, 1921"

I would like to thank the MacDowell Colony and the Robert Frost Place, where some of these poems were written, for their support.

For Brad

How should I praise Thee, Lord! how should my rhymes
   Gladly engrave Thy love in steel
If, what my soul doth feel sometimes,
   My soul might ever feel!

               —George Herbert, "The Temper"

CONTENTS

I

II

III

I

FOR AN ITALIAN COUSIN

Mia cugina, with the black-olive eyes,
escorts me arm-in-arm through her church,
leads me from saint to saint in search
of the chapel where the Savior lies.
"Ah," she sighs, and pulls back the drape,
exposing Him rose-strewn, pink and yellow—
Easter colors. *"Non è bello?"*
she whispers, seeing my mouth agape.
His wounds look fresh, but it's not this sight
that shocks me so much as His man-made skin:
He's waxen, slick as a mannequin.
Good Friday, she says, tomorrow night,
all the young men, each wearing a crown
of thorns and white gloves, as every year,
will march to funeral music and bear
on high His body through the town.

To simplify, I'm a *protestante*.
But this, she tells me in careful Italian,
is called the Catholic religion.
You know of this? You have read some Dante?
Tempted to joke, I'm silenced by
the trusting expression on her face,
flushed with the light of this stained glass
where Christ is always about to die.

I could say, from a place that seldom admits
such light—the world I bring with me—

these writhing thieves in agony
affect me more than the crucifix
of His body, limp and white. And yet again
I'd show you, *cugina*, a world I've pieced
together with a kind of faith, at least:
in San Marco in Venice, where you've never been,
you stand on patterns on patterns of tiles
and discover, above, the roseate tones
flowering in each face are stones
hard as the pillars in the aisles.
A puzzle of figures floats on the walls
and in golden domes, and you have the feeling
this heavenly gold is not a ceiling—
but space itself, from which no one falls.

REFRAIN

But let his disposition have that scope
As dotage gives it.
                    —Goneril to Albany

Never afflict yourself to know the cause,
said Goneril, her mind already set.
No one can tell us who her mother was

or, knowing, could account then by the laws
of nurture for so false and hard a heart.
Never afflict yourself to know the cause

of Lear's undoing: if without a pause
he shunned Cordelia, as soon he saw the fault.
No one can tell us who her mother was,

but here's a pretty reason seven stars
are seven stars: because they are not eight.
Never afflict yourself to know the cause—

like servants, even one's superfluous.
The King makes a good fool: the Fool is right.
No one can tell him who his mother was

when woman's water-drops are all he has
against the storm, and daughters cast him out.
Never afflict yourself to know the cause;
no one can tell you who your mother was.

"OFFICER AND LAUGHING GIRL"

Light falls from the left. Or so
it falls in the chambers of Vermeer,
as even now in this office, where

a six-by-nine glossy print is tacked
above a desk, high in a city
that has no place on the valanced map

on the wall of the painted girl. The quaint
sprawl of that projected shape
is another world she's never seen—

no, apparently she's seen not much
of anything, the laughing girl
who sits an arm's length away,

a window's width of sun, from the faceless
officer. Who can deny,
studying them, the historical rift

in every experience of the sexes?
The back of his jaunty hat, the black
space-arrogating nerve of it;

and the puffed-up crimson sleeve he cocks
behind in our direction, the fist
curling at the hip, and the wrist

enveloped in the flounce of his blouse.
The sun-dazzled oval of her face
tilts, just so, in a border of starched

white scarf; and her hands, as if to hold
off some possibility,
circle a glinting, long-stemmed glass

from which, it appears, she has yet to drink.
Crystalline, her eyes reflect
on him: it's clear he told the joke.

MARY CAZZATO, 1921

I

She's lovely—though the photograph
   I've kept of her is not
of anyone I knew. Eighteen
back then, in nineteen twenty-one,
and in her rickrack headband, half-
   flapper, maybe. But

at her ear, a Victorian rose
   speaks more of what she was,
or would become to me—as yet,
my grandfather remains unmet.
(She'd had no thought of us at all;
   and yet would make us feel

we were the reason *she* was here—
   as if, engendered, love's
the engenderer.) She was born, for me,
sometime around nineteen sixty,
already wearing lace-trimmed gloves;
   a lady playing poker.

Strange how it all starts to condense—
   the only song I can
recall her playing on that spinet
"My Bonnie Lies Over the Ocean";
those childhood dances on her carpet
   resolve into one dance.

II

Pregnant with our deaths (a germ
    within the mind suspects),
we carry their date and kind with us
like the embryo's blind sex,
regardless of our ignorance,
    for a life's full term.

Yet who's to say the future's not
    a table laid in haste
for every unexpected guest?
Still blooming, the bouquet that winds
and spills over her tiny hands
    seems then to tumble out

of the frame wherein, expressionless,
    she evenly can face
everything she's yet to lose:
the suicide of the brother whose
wedding this is, and even the freak
    event that turned a shock

of her hair, at thirty-two, all white:
    the skidding truck that killed
one whose very name was blessed,
Angela Paradise, her child.
She lost two in her grief: Grandmother
    had been carrying another.

III

I was barely older, when she died,
   than the girl whose portrait clicks
shut like a coffin in my palm.
Black velvet's on the other side.
—Years later, a recurrent dream:
   she winks at me and looks

as though there's something to disclose,
   but first, we climb long stairs,
the two of us, to a sunny room I'd
swear I knew—those olive chairs;
dropped in a crystal vase, a rose.
   I'd forgotten that she's dead—

she doesn't say so . . . but one knows.
   And vacantly her eyes
hold nothing of my own surprise.
Shrugging ("What did you suppose?"),
she's gone—and leaves behind a locket
   enfolding one last secret

between two views the living can't
   connect: the thoughtless stare
of the girl, and the perpetual black
unblinkingly regarding her.
There's never time to call her back—
   to ask her what she meant.

ON READING A WRITER'S LETTERS

At last we have a picture of her life—
more colorful than honest, as her trade
led her to value more the thing that's made
than what it's made of. One must wonder if
even a scribbled postcard's a first draft,
knowing the curse that forced her to revise;
and once she coined a phrase, she spent it twice.
Her correspondents variously were left

with lines of a character nobody knew
wholly except herself, perhaps, whose talent
shows finally that self in overview:
she is this artifice, we'd say, if we
her readers, unacquainted but omniscient
narrators, were asked to tell her story.

JOHN LENNON

I

The music was already turning sad,
   those fresh-faced voices singing in a round
      the lie that time could set its needle back

and play from the beginning. Had you lived
   to eighty, as you'd wished, who knows?—you might
      have broken from the circle of that past

more ours than yours. Never even sure
   which was the truest color for your hair
      (it changed with each photographer), we claimed

you for ourselves; called you John and named
   the day you left us (spun out like a reel—
      the last broadcast to prove you'd lived at all)

an end to hope itself. It isn't true,
   and worse, does you no justice if we call
      your death the death of anything but you.

II

It put you in the headlines once again:
   years after you'd left the band, you joined
      another—of those whose lives, in breaking, link

all memory with their end. The studio
   of history can tamper with you now,
      as if there'd always been a single track

chance traveled on, and your discordant voice
    had led us to the final violence.
        Yet like the times when I, a star-crossed fan,

had catalogued your favorite foods, your views
    on monarchy and war, and gaily clipped
        your quips and daily antics from the news,

I keep a loving record of your death.
    All the evidence is in—of what,
        and to what end, it's hard to figure out,

riddles you might have beat into a song.
    A younger face of yours, a cover shot,
        peered from all the newsstands as if proof

of some noteworthy thing you'd newly done.

LUMINARY

Just *how* did she come to be there—
shining hugely, inches above the street,
like the answer risen from a question?
In a moment's movement, between
long rows of houses with an air
of subjects at attention,
she settled all her weight
on a great, invisible throne.

For hours the traffic, like the one-
way tide of her desire,
was drawn into that signal stare.
Yet as she rose she dwindled; what
had seemed the dazzling crown
of a sun-descended sovereign
contracted to a pillbox hat
morning would pull down.

Retiring rather late that night,
although still a queen, she fit
into the grid of one windowpane
the size of a chessboard square.
And with room to spare—
enough to allow a pawn
among the advancing stars to share
the spot she rested on.

ON REMOVING SUMMER
FROM THE PUBLIC GARDENS

—Geraniums, weren't they? And
was it yesterday that x'd
their exhuming? Another
summer gone, and autumn brings

its reproachful litany:
you'll never learn botany,
you'll never learn Latin. What's
happened to the gardener

who held summer in such high
esteem? Working bare-chested
even in rain, but driven
by the calendar like hay-

fever or horseflies, he must
have bundled up his tools, and
headed south with the birds. Now
a squirrel quivers a tail

of smoke, serving himself one
acorn in its own brown bowl;
from the pond, where ducks and Swan
Boats paddled in currents of

their own making, gapes a silence
not of frozen water, but

no water at all. The drained
tub, whose gradient is such

leaves beach on its rim like fish,
is deep enough to suggest
a moat between you and things
you see coming; the trumped-up

island of earth, rock and tree
could be a lion's turf—zoo
for the predator, raw-eyed
Winter, pacing and staring.

THE SEASON OF METAPHOR

We've finally turned up the thermostat,
but as we wait shivering for the heat,
it's our other senses that
confirm a change in the weather:
the smell, like a rain-dampened sweater's,
of lukewarm grime—for at first,
the dusty shells of themselves are all
the radiators steam. From room
to room they commence a snappish,
testy chorus, which allows no rest
until it has called up such suggestions
as a tennis warm-up, a rap
at the door, the arrhythmic clank-clank
of popcorn against the fryer's lid.
Then we hear water . . . in the kitchen, the miserly
trickle of a campsite shower; in the bedroom,
the wheezy whistle of a tea-kettle;
in the nursery, a hot-water bottle
emptying with a gush, then a sputter.
Soon all resemblance to water
evaporates: in the study, two cars
with all the lackluster bluster of Edsels
are racing through their gears.

It hardly seems important,
and we try to set our minds
on other matters. Only as we forget
how cold we were a moment ago,
before the air took on the taste
of another indoor winter,

does the reason for this game
come to the tongue.
                              Now we've begun
the season of metaphor, when the very
idea of heat and light
must approximate something of summer,
and we're liars like Huck Finn—
who, when Tom Sawyer kicked a gun
in his sleep, explained: "He had a dream,
and it shot him." If winter's not cold
and green not gone, it's only because things pass
through memory first, and wrapped
in the warm, plush jacket
of likeness, recall to us
simply the body's honest
craving for the sun.

INCH BY INCH

Small hollows in streets
brim full and flatten;
an open-mouthed mailbox
begins to fatten.

Inside-out, showing seams
or skeletons
(the lines of a dress
or long white bones),

what's upright remains
touched barely, but rimmed
like a plan of itself:
a house snow-trimmed.

Though you read the arches
on the tops of cars,
or window-sills against
perpendiculars

as the blizzard's index,
watch how, inch by inch,
each profile distorts
as the blowing lifts:

evergreens extend
white-gloved bear paws,
a bare bush grows
buds of pussywillows,

and the wind in drifts
leaves a mound of powder,
a heap like a cat
at the foot of your door.

HERB

For I will consider my kitten, Herb.
There's nothing in the house he won't disturb
except the toy mouse I bought him—apparently, a bore.
He'd far rather stalk the dustballs on the floor.

What cat, I ask, is better treated?
He's napped an hour now in my lap, but is he
happy? Not until I stroke him dizzy—
or he shoots me the look of someone who's been cheated.

The worlds he'll never comprehend!
Just because *he* does, he thinks I should spend
all my days sleeping and causing trouble.
But his standards, by anyone's standards, are double;

for it seems to me, Herb, that even at your age
you can tell when a person's busy. And you ought
to see (since I'm writing *your* story) that it's not
productive to walk, or nibble, on the page—

especially since I'd planned to add
your influence here has not been wholly bad.
You've given me an eye for the tiny spaces
between things, which I never saw as places:

the day I brought you home, the top
of the bookcase seemed an obvious spot to hop,

but you had a fine conception of size and self—
you slipped between the first and second shelf.

A head-first spelunker, you plumb the ridge
between the mountainous cushions on the couch,
and with plenty of room to spare—but no, not much—
will claim the slit of dark behind the Fridge,

poking your face out when I worry.
Those not as young as you, Herb, have to hurry
if we are to make hay of our brief time.
But though I must expect you'll whine and climb

all over your next owner, and wait
as impatiently as ever for love and fish,
I want you to accept a heartfelt wish:
be joyous in this life, and your next eight.

BEE'S ELEGY

Smashing a bee
with a book,
I shuddered; then
shuddered again—
to think murder
occurred in this small
ball of fur.

I'd tried to save
the damn thing;
flung open windows
to let it go—
as open as my heart,
I wanted it
to know.

But a bug this size
has no eyes for
metaphor; nor
could it seize
on the current
of thought in the room's
new breeze.

Bumbling about,
it would have traced
one spot of wall

all afternoon.
Like the lemon
whose fragrance once
so stung my nose

it wrung
from me all sense
but smell,
the yellow buzz
of life beneath
my swoop crushed me
enough to tell.

AMPHITHEATER WITH TREES

Hidden in woods, but not a secret
(the pagan and artistic set
nearby considers it enshrined),
an amphitheater, designed
seventy years ago for use
by the local Drama Club, has since
fallen into disrepair.
Cropping up as spectators,
each of these young, stone-splitting trees
pays heed in varying degrees:

some casual, snapped maples slouch
across four rows, while a stand of birch
rises in ovation; and a spruce
lingers in rapt audience,
rooted by things yet to begin.
Onstage, a chorus in evergreen
silence, a *corps de ballet* well-cast
by seedings of the recent past,
awaits directions in tableau.
Odd, isn't it? and still the show

seems ancient. Nobody needs to ask
what's lying behind the thicket's mask—

like a dream which, if no simple word
could describe its mystery, is less absurd
than it is a re-fashioned memory.
Once, you could as easily say,
there were people playing trees. In Rome,
standing in the abandoned Forum,
you might see a decimated forest,
uncertain as to which comes first.

FACSIMILE OF A CHAPEL

Having taken in showrooms
done up à la Louis Quatorze,
and admired countless inlays
of wood, fine porcelain pitchers,
velvet-brocaded curtains heavy
with their own ratty history; having pondered
the sixty-eight-pound suit some poor
knight wore to the wars, and a large gay Buddha
whose paint has not yet faded,
three *stanze* of Italian blue-and-red
Madonnas, and it seems hundreds
of Crucifixions in which angels float
(their bodies in profile one simple
wing) beneath the Savior's wrists
to salvage his blood in pots,

I found tucked away, in one
corner of the museum,
a facsimile of a chapel. Although
its walls weren't hewn of stone, but poured
into sheet rock, and its "pews"
were the fold-up kind, in case
everything should have to be shifted,
surely it was as much a chapel
as the one now closed at the local airport,

which had interested vandals mainly, and taken
no more time to erect than any
syndicated architecture
devoted to the hamburger.

As it always does when I forget
I'm not really a Christian, my heart
flew to my knees. I was praying,
once again, for the soul
of my grandmother. Behind the stained
and glorious glass ("French: 12th century")
calculated to provoke exactly
this genius of heart, or infirmity, which takes
all beauty for truth, out there in the non-
air-conditioned air, the hot
traffic improvised its aimless
music, and whole colonies
of artists were being born to decry
the notion of beauty itself.

What consecrates a place? Although
the chapel was largely French-and-12th, a bit
of Spain was thrown in, and some 13th.
Thinking not of the faithful
craftsmen who fashioned the cross, the glass,

the altarpiece, but more
of the movers who shipped them here
(and more of the magnificence
of the Curator than the Creator)
it was difficult to feel sure
of a holy presence. But isn't God everywhere?

Or nowhere? In the cold light of reason
(above the stained glass, track-
lights one might find in a modern kitchen),
I thought of that blindered, overbearing knight.
I wouldn't have brought back his Crusades,
wouldn't confess to sins that don't
originate with me.
               Yet knowing of my share,
and knowing I'd never happen, in my own
century, on a place better to look,
I pulled up a chair.

ANTHROPOD

There's nothing green,
it would seem, in the past
of this petrified pod,
stuffed until burst-
ing cotton from wood;
it is so human,

how far a thing ends
from where it began.
As though it's blown
out its brains, it stands
bobbing, the neck
a quarter-inch thick;

but (this is odd)
the tip of each lock
of baby-hair's tied
with seeds strung on sheer
ribbons of air.
One brown plume in back,

one salted birdtail
of intransigent leaf,
yet postures as if

what passes for dead
needs a hat—and may well
be alive; for milkweed

runs its own kind of blood.
When a breeze comes to split
top from stalk, the snap
releases instead
a slow, gummy sap:
it's chillingly white.

TWO PIGEONS

They've perched for hours
on that window-ledge, scarcely
moving. Beak to beak,

a matched set, they differ
almost imperceptibly—
like salt and pepper shakers.

It's an event when they tuck
(simultaneously) their pinpoint
heads into lavender vests

of fat. But reminiscent
of clock hands blandly
turning because they must

have turned—somehow, they've
taken on the grave,
small-eyed aspect of monks

hooded in conferences
so intimate nothing need
be said. If some are chuckling

in the park, earning
their bread, these are content
to let the dark engulf them—

it's all the human
imagination can fathom,
how single-mindedly

mindless two silhouettes
stand in a window thick
as milk glass. They appear

never to have fed on
anything else when they stir
all of a sudden to peck

savagely, for love
or hygiene, at the grimy
feathers of the other;

but when they resume
their places, the shift
is one only a painter

or a barber (prodding a chin
back into position)
would be likely to notice.

ROCKY HARBOUR, NEWFOUNDLAND

How disastrous it looks—
the rust washed into the rocks,
and the wrecked ship itself, picked clean.
It was 1911
when the Evangeline beached here,
a leviathan at Rocky Harbour;
and all the accidents since, the deadlier
figures of bodies, falling, afire,
cannot extinguish the primeval
power, like a monumental
skull's, of a hull
the seas coldly rejected. Not content
to leave it lying, bent
on reducing it now to an element
of itself, the omnivorous water hurls
its weight on the gutted belly; and hissing, curls
its white fingers back, and pulls.

But whatever it reclaims
is invisible now that the frame's
becoming simply another stark
contour on the shoreline: an ark
divested of animals, foreign trinkets,
sailors or (in this case) families on junkets
round the Gulf of St. Lawrence,
and eroding—though with a sense

of the dramatic—toward what could be an odd
rock that resembles a ship, as a cloud
might pass for a sheep or whale.

No one could miss the DANGER—all
the signs proclaim it—
but there may be some doubt as to what
the Preservationists hope to avert:
any harm to child-scavengers
scaling the beams, or the disaster's
loss of its intact
and forbidding message. How astonishing then
to encounter in fine
print the overlooked fact
that the disaster's not one
at all. Not one
of the passengers, numbering sixty-seven,
perished; not even the baby
posted ashore in a mailbag. Maybe
any such delivery
from evil is apocryphal, but a detail
so painstakingly improbable
is rarely wrong;
and who knows? we too may be numbered among
the legendary company of the delivered.

II

ENGLAND

At times it seemed the country itself was a cloud
high up on the map, a sheepwool shape in the sea
that might as easily rise to break blue sky.
But meadows dipped beneath rough cows and horses;
rippled with short-fur grass, the scruff of earth.

As if, like me, they longed to come in early,
the cold days shrank from darkness.
I pedaled home uphill and saw the light
foreshorten, felt my beaded breath fall back.

Those mornings I would wake to watch the leaves rain.
Too damp to burn, their colors ran and blurred,
turning a mottled surface underneath.
Seeped in a world as kind as my intentions,
through miles of glass and cloud, I thought of you.

LOVE POEM FOR A POET

For reasons we could never see as clear,
    I left you for a year.
     My first week back I paged
Through you, each paragraph,
     As if to find exact
    Endearments held from a letter,
But found, perhaps, something better—
     The vague, painful whole of fact
    Forgotten. I can't say we've "aged,"
     Although we have . . . you'd laugh.

But home this time, I suddenly remember
     One Thanksgiving break
    You spent alone at my place
As if camped out for November.
     I wondered if you knew
    As you took me back with kisses
How grateful I was, too—
     For your shaken, unshaven face.
    "Look, I've washed your dishes,"
     You said, and for my sake

You'd also not replaced them on the shelf—
     But, so that I might see
    Your interest that all life
Dishevel like yourself,
     Cleanly and openly,
    You'd set the plates to dry
On chair-arms, stove-top, floor.
     You're still like this: each drawer

Ajar; notes left for my eye
        From a girl almost your wife.

I see now what I'd ignored before, drawn
        To know everything of you:
        Knowledge we have a right to
But hurts us, we think is forbidden
        Even to ourselves. . . . The book
    Of our own lives we spy on
With an ethic we shouldn't look.
        With you, I find all's hidden
        Though it's brought up from the deep.
        Even when you sleep:

Too preoccupied to find the light
        Or paper, late at night
        You scribbled new stray lines
On the wall above your bed—
        Sometimes a little under
        If the thought ran on—
In letters fit for road-signs
        Or others (I still wonder,
        Did you stand up on your head?)
        Insect-size and upside-down.

Didn't Michelangelo sketch "cartoons"
        On *his* jail walls? That isn't,
        You would say, the same . . .
But these scrawled thought-balloons
        Remind me you're imprisoned

By art, as I am by love:
I scan the words above
     Your pillowed head for a "she"
That might, or might not, be me;
     I even look for my name.

I tell myself these words, like any kind
     Of exposure of your mind,
     Are only half the picture—
To decipher what lies here
     Is not to comprehend yet
How you might use it.
But I go on prying.
     It's jealousy, but not
Of what you might have thought;
     Even you were trying,

I saw the other night, to transcribe cryptic
     Notes onto a pad
     As if, shaking your head,
You wanted me to glean
     What you had meant to mean.
It's the turn of your elliptic
Brain that stings me. Smitten,
     I'm crushed by every fear
     I guess is yours. . . . I've written
     You about it. Here.

FIRST SNOW IN
CAMBRIDGE, ENGLAND

I bring us a steaming pot
of tea on a tray
(your favorite: Earl Grey).
Happier than
I can explain, I play

Jeeves to your Wooster willingly.
Wodehouse seems
to us the proper thing
on a morning
that extends itself all day;

young though we are, we take
for a god
this man who produced one book
a year for each
of his ninety-odd.

No such hero is Bertie.
Sipping tea,
you read aloud his bedded
breakfast: "I tucked
into the eggs and b." . . .

How does the snow induce
such indolence?
So clear a cold in this year

of mere mist and chill,
snow falls as if it means to—

lies like the crust of sun
that whitened the tops
of leaves last summer, a green
so bright it was gone.
Why does it seem

that today we must begin
and begin again?
Hot cereal for breakfast,
a lunch of eggs,
pancakes and milk for dinner.

As if it's not our first
day snowbound here,
but the last of this dark year
in which "one can pretend
one needn't care

what one shall ever do,"
we take a cue
that white is what we're after:
thin-skinned, we lie
awake and under cover.

AT CITY HALL

"What kind of license you looking for?"
the woman lounging behind
the counter asked. What *kind*?
A question so disarming the groom

(just outvoicing the dusty carriage
wheels of ceiling fans)
conceded ignorance. "Don't mind
him," the bride said. "A marriage

license." Across the room,
the only sign—and it was huge—
was lettered, simply, DOG LICENSES.
A routine mix-up, doubtless,

as this must be as well: "First
time for both?" The reply—a check
in the box provided, size of a thumbtack,
on a page with room for

marriages of the future—
applied equally to the best and worst
of intentions. As he supplied their proof
of blood, of residence, of birth,

she held her pen above
a line marked "Married Name": for who

she was, and what of She was He,
was not to be resolved

by closing time. Meanwhile, her
first footprint for signature,
no bigger than a cat's paw, he
paused to get the gist of. She

who on all his life to come
had laid a claim—staggering
in its singleness
of purpose—had once

been living, evidently,
only for minutes. . . Asked now to raise
right hands, to swear they knew
of no impediment,

he set down his tennis racket;
their eyes, for an instant long
to be remembered, gravely met
in the sweet embrace of fear.

EXPECTANCY
(Japan Baptist Hospital, Kyoto)

One by one, we shuffle in
and take a quiet seat beneath
admonitory posters. Here's
Mrs. Shimoda, who, to judge from
her pink, quilted jumper appliquéd
with rabbits, and a fuzzy, enormous purse
emblazoned with cartoon characters,

appears to be in some confusion
as to whether she's going to have a baby
or (a greater miracle) become one;
and here's sorrowful Mrs. Fukumoto,
who hasn't looked well in weeks. Of course
I'm guessing—I'm a newcomer here,
and as the nurse calls out each name

just a touch louder than necessary
in a kindly, patronizing singsong,
I flinch. Thermometer under tongue,
blood pressure measured, I can clearly see
a needle creeping on the hateful scale
where serene Mrs. Oh, five months along,
checks in at less than I at two.

Yet don't I, in fact, want to feel the weight
of waiting once again? the way
(years ago) each birthday took years to arrive . . .

Oh to be sixteen at last, to drive,
to come home past eleven! To loosen
the hold of parents who'd grown to fear
time as a thing they only got less of,

while you knew, yourself, it was stored within.
Too early, I know, I begin to imagine
how the baby turns in its own waiting room,
as restlessly as I now turn
a health-book page in a half-learned language:
Let's guard against (illegible);
be sure to (illegible) *every day!*

But here's the man who can read it all:
the doctor—handsome, young, a bit proud,
as if the father of all our children—
billows in on a white, open-coated sail
and, bowing to us with nautical
briskness, takes the time to wish
the mates a benevolent good morning.

We murmur in kind; then, in a hush,
some dozen heads in unison
swivel to follow his form until
it vanishes behind a door.
Daily, I think, women just like us

are found normal there. Who shall be the first?
It's Mrs. Hino—although the nurse

has to call her twice, across the length
of eight abstracted months. She rises
slowly, resting, in a universal
gesture I've only begun to read,
one hand on the swell below her breasts
as though what's borne within
were here, and could be taken in her arms.

JAPANESE CHARACTERS

I

To look into a word as through a window
and address the thing itself: a simple wish,
and one calling me to a simpler time—
yet when can that have been? Life before English?
Conversant in the automatic doors
of an alphabet we barely need to press
for meaning sprung wide-open, now it seems
that again to sound things out and memorize
new, ramifying claims upon the eyes
is, piece by piece, to reconstruct a cosmos
I'd grown to think long set and spoken for.
Just as all life appears to have begun
the moment we were born, so around the sun
of native language orbit distant bodies
in atmospheres indigenously vague:
seen as through clouds, that's Venus thickly wrapped
in idioms colorful and yet inapt,
and Saturn's ring spins far too fast to wear.

The untold ideographs of Japanese
were Chinese first. To them are grafted two
syllabaries, native and phonetic,
which cling to borrowed roots. It grows aesthetic
to gaze upon these fruitless branchings, gnarled
so intricately no one in the world
can paint them right except a Japanese.
—Or so they'd have you think. Riding the bus,
my breath fogged on the pane, I puzzled out

streets whose billboards lettered in a scrawl
news that the world had slipped out of control.
Like insects some mad scientist had bred
to overrun an old, bad movie made
here in Japan, these characters were bound
to do us in. . . Enchanted, terrified,
at first I'd spend whole days cooped up behind
my room's milk-tinted glass. So little choice—
to view the brighter goings-on below
only by sliding free long streets of noise,
or to muffle them, but dim the light at once.

To look into a word as through a window
entirely clear—I'd given up that chance;
filmed over with the past, our TV screen
gave out on movies we'd already seen
at home. They'd been dubbed in Japanese,
but stubbornly, I felt as though I could
stare down the actors, coax them to unearth
my language lurking voiceless underneath.
Even at theaters, where we could hear
English so sharp we hung upon its edge,
characters white on black, and black on white
("subtitles" to the side, as hieroglyphic
as the crabbed marginalia on a page)
transported us to an unfeatured age
—past or future? it was hard to say—where night
is never clear enough to chart the stars.

II

It's typhoon season. Above, a paper-thin
sky fills with figured clouds: an inky wash
the wind reconsiders swiftly with its brush.
Below, low-lying thunderheads (a queue
of black-haired students decked in navy blue,
each topped—like a dream of sun—with a yellow hat)
now and again burst out in laughter. Yet
they keep their civic files and parallels
that (paradoxically) might better suit
the strict march of our destined-to-repeat,
typecast, upstanding roman ABC's
whose measured zones our children (in their note-
books ruled like music staves) can fill
with nothing but the obsessive English trill.
How is it that the straitened Japanese,
living by Muzak and the megaphone,
tossed from such boats of reference stay afloat
with strokes on their letters fluent as a stream,
always familiar, never quite the same?
A mystery even when, some damp weeks later,
these start to take on clues of . . . character.

Each I could set apart from all the rest
began to stalk me—as, once, a night of cards
turned every dream to numerals for words,
and every one called out to be the last:
after I'd run through King and Jack and Queen,

thousands of faces beckoned me for names,
thousands of names for faces yet unseen.
Old women, bent at pained diagonals
like orchid grass; others in Western chairs
asquat on pliant feet, so that four legs
of wood then stood in place of two of theirs—
stamped on my brain as whole and legible
at last, they seemed to press a further claim
on life's behalf: *you're here to crack the code.*
In whiteface, wig, kimono, here's a Bride.
The Guests need not be guessed: identified
as men in black suits, ties of white brocade,
women in black kimono with a hem
brushed with bamboo or crane. They carry gifts
the right size for *furoshiki*, a square
of wrapping cloth that's often lavender.
Let there be no mistaking what we are,
they seem to say, *it's chaos otherwise;*
we'll limit human types to memorize.

III

One day in the paper, there's a story
on an amateur astronomer— a factory
worker who, gazing on the stars
just before dawn with plain binoculars
("a part of my routine patrol," he said),
spotted a nova no one else had found.
"I know the sky quite well, but this was luck,"

he told reporters, "to catch it at its peak"—
three minutes of intensity before
a star we wake to think the only one
blotted with light all light except its own.

"I know the sky quite well"— a vivid claim
suggesting a nightly rummage through its shelves
of scorpions and saucepans. We ourselves
can't hope to re-arrange the stars, but name
and name again, as if to cut to size
chaos that takes us hugely by surprise.
Like stars, like snow . . . when clusters of words come,
some melt, a disappointment, on the tongue,
their mystery gone—and yet their calligraphic
descent to comprehension followed traffic
down streets untraceable on any map.
And in sculptured garden-ponds, I now expect
bridges of stepstones one line can't connect,
grammar reversing like a velvet nap
whose shade of meaning fades upon my touch. . .
Gravity's upended. The universe
observes, it seems, the old misspeller's curse:
You have to have things down to look them up.

What am I learning, then? Perhaps to wish
less fervently the Romans will march in
dispensing justice: for every man one vote,
for every voice a single character.
(What should we call the lanes between the stars,

or the silence burning even at the cores
of those so bright they make us feverish?)
Just as new words, once never seen, appear
on every page as soon as known, the sky
prints images upon the clouded eye:
distinguish these, and others will come clear.
Immersed in truths by half, the vertigo
of apprehending patterns through a window
rinsed clean—until it may well not be there—
one questions further. "What's next to the Bear?"

WELCOME TO HIROSHIMA

is what you first see, stepping off the train:
a billboard brought to you in living English
by Toshiba Electric. While a channel
silent in the TV of the brain

projects those flickering re-runs of a cloud
that brims its risen columnful like beer
and, spilling over, hangs its foamy head,
you feel a thirst for history: what year

it started to be safe to breathe the air,
and when to drink the blood and scum afloat
on the Ohta River. But no, the water's clear,
they pour it for your morning cup of tea

in one of the countless sunny coffee shops
whose plastic dioramas advertise
mutations of cuisine behind the glass:
a pancake sandwich; a pizza someone tops

with a maraschino cherry. Passing by
the Peace Park's floral hypocenter (where
how bravely, or with what mistaken cheer,
humanity erased its own erasure),

you enter the memorial museum
and through more glass are served, as on a dish
of blistered grass, three mannequins. Like gloves
a mother clips to coatsleeves, strings of flesh

hang from their fingertips; or as if tied
to recall a duty for us, *Reverence*
the dead whose mourners too shall soon be dead,
but all commemoration's swallowed up

in questions of bad taste, how re-created
horror mocks the grim original,
and thinking at last *They should have left it all*
you stop. This is the wristwatch of a child.

Jammed on the moment's impact, resolute
to communicate some message, although mute,
it gestures with its hands at eight-fifteen
and eight-fifteen and eight-fifteen again

while tables of statistics on the wall
update the news by calling on a roll
of tape, death gummed on death, and in the case
adjacent, an exhibit under glass

is glass itself: a shard the bomb slammed in
a woman's arm at eight-fifteen, but some
three decades on—as if to make it plain
hope's only as renewable as pain,

and as if all the unsung
debasements of the past may one day come
rising to the surface once again—
worked its filthy way out like a tongue.

HENRY PURCELL IN JAPAN

Here death does not confine itself
to the shuttered funeral parlor,
but roams from house to house like a beggar,
as quotidian as rain.
Today, once again, I saw them queuing
(the tail-coated men, black birds on a line,
the women columnar in kimono)
at a door where death had visited.
High bamboo placards draped in white
but muddied with sweeping characters
(names, perhaps, of those left behind)
were propped against the tiny house
like rafts secured to a bank.
Yet no one was going anywhere,

not the men whose task was to register
at felt-covered tables, brilliant red,
whatever was to be registered,
nor the women who made themselves at home
serving cups of pale green tea.
As I walked by they stared at me—
not angry, not stirring or saying a word,
but as if they expected me to concede
I didn't belong there. I remembered how,
standing in a Buddhist graveyard
some months ago—overseen by a crow

enormously foreign, and called *karasu*—
I'd known I was a trespasser.

It was their names that told me:
names recalled with unspeakable grace,
the chiseled letters liquid in stone
as if by brushwork. Reading down,
I felt as though the ashes of someone
whose name ran vertically might lie
differently, somehow, in the earth.
Such a small note seemed everything—
as today, once home from the funeral,
I listened to a choir sing Henry Purcell.
Rejoice in the Lord alway,
they sang; *And again I say rejoice!*
How explain to anyone the joy
of that single missing "s"—a winding path

down into a heritage so deep,
so long a part of me it seems
the very state of God?
The mellow, antiquated light
of drafty English chapels, and the comfort
of harmonies layered against the cold—
how exchange this god, like money,
for whatever imbues a Shinto shrine

painted the orange and gold of fire
with a bell-rung spirit more austere?
No, surely they were right,
the mourners who stared at me today;
schooled in other mysteries,
I stood as far from them

(or so it felt) as we all stood
from the foreign country of the dead.
Yet at home in my random corner
on truth, with no choice but to play
the world sung in a transposed key,
mine was another mourner's voice:
And again I say rejoice.

AT THE PUBLIC BATHS
(Kyoto, 1982)

Not many of her kind left,
she has to know, unwrapping the *obi*
sash from about her gray kimono,
a daily, unthinking ritual.
Another decade, two, they will be gone
who find this costume natural,
and in only months the newborn baby
fussing in a basket (lacquered
straw, and made for folding clothes in)
will have outgrown his tiny playpen.

Yet tonight it's coming down to this
shared moment for the two of them—
Grandmother cooing *hai, hai, hai,*
yes yes, she's heard it all before,
as she lifts, then plunges him with rough
certitude he'll survive into water
heart-stoppingly hot;
the infant shrunk to one blood-red cry
who learns, or will soon enough,
this is the way things are.

Under the ticking reel of ceiling
fans that slice fluorescent light
into sputtering frames, we lunge and jerk

like characters in a vintage movie,
while a Casablancan, ever-rising
mist calls up the queerest feeling
of having slipped into the past.
Although a sweating wallclock tells
real time, the homely black-and-white
of its method looks antique

as last year's fifteen-year-old starlet
who waves from an unturned calendar.
Even the ads naively painted
on mirrors—for fresh octopus,
bed shops or billiards—and a "Western"-style
mural in alpine blue on tile
you might call "Heidi Comes to Mt. Fuji"
seem to illustrate the past's
entirely arbitrary, yet
settled, claims on us who live it.

Slid fast to shut the foggy bath
from the dressing room, a cut-glass door
of Fuji again (this time ascended
by a ladder of philosophic clouds)
in patches of clarity affords
the unrestricted view—
if not divine, at least aerial

and impossibly particular—
we're sometimes given of the earth
as a place where nothing's wholly ended,

but disappears in stages. Staggered
across another day with him,
a steaming bundle that she tucks
beneath one arm, Grandmother locks
their baskets into cupboards with a key
carved with not-strictly-necessary
grapevines. *Say goodbye to the baby?*
another mother calls to her laggard
daughter who, though no more than two,
knows enough to bow.

AMONG THE *NINGYO*

(*ningyō*: a doll; literally, "human form")

It is the third of March,
and in houses shut against the sun—
the windows tinted, barred, the gardens
cloistered deep within
a courtyard, or behind high walls,
meant to be looked on rather than
stepped out to—on thin, constricted streets
like this, throughout Japan,

today's the *Hina Matsuri*,
the Girls' Doll Festival. On shelves
wherever they've been found a space,
a seated Emperor and Empress
(feet tucked under hips, a fan
in hand) this week have been
drowsily hosting all, their eyes
narrow islets of bliss.

Her own brows, plucked, then newly drawn
like falsetto notes just shy
of the hairline, are her only
indication of surprise
at having again been resurrected
from the Heian Era of a thousand
years ago and more—
days when people were upholstered

masses of padded silk, and ladies
wore twelve kimono at once.
Each hem shorter than the one

beneath, her figured robes balloon,
slips too gorgeous not to show;
on her head a chandelier
of a crown confirms the sense that she's
herself a kind of furniture.

Yes . . . she'd be soft enough to sleep on,
she and her thickly bundled husband
(as petite as she, but in a hat
like a snake's tongue, or a flame
leaping up to claim supremacy),
if it weren't that everything
has been perfectly arranged already,
the quilted layers of *futon*

(folded again and again, until
they're nearly two inches high)
set out atop the lacquered chests
within which, one believes,
more bedding yet is stored, enough
for everybody. It's like "The Twelve
Days of Christmas," with all
these courtiers on step-like shelves

(three maids a-serving, five
ministers a-bowing) and all
the accoutrements of luxury
(the gilded flutes, the tea-bowls fine
as eggshells, even an ox-drawn cart
with wheels of pounded damascene)

arrayed below like ornaments
on a branching, laden pine.

It's this expansiveness
they breathe, the unthinking, vast expense
of space that is their greatest wealth—
the way their lives lie open
as scenes from the *Tale of Genji* scrolls,
where kneeling women behind folding
screens are at last exposed to light,
overseen as in a doll's

house whose roof's been lifted off.
Yet tomorrow, and on other mornings
soon, the looming, sorry clouds
of real girls' hands will reach
to dismantle like a Christmas tree
the fabulous display
there won't again be such room for
until this time next March.

SHISENDŌ
(The Hall of the Hermit-Poets)

Only the first time will it seem so easy
to know where to begin—
at the outer gate, of course, at the open
and unshuttable view of a rocky flight of steps.
Bamboo-leaf breaks its shadows on the rocks
like a spoon dropped in a glass of water.
Yet even this may not be the proper start;
here in the northeast hills, first you must climb
until Kyoto shrinks within the palm
at the base of one long, narrow arm of street
to reach the site where Ishikawa Jōzan
retreated from the feudal wars, and built
the hermitage whose gate now stands ajar.

This time, once again, it is autumn, and dusk
seems not to be something falling, but a rose
and slate-blue smoke that levitates from rooftops,
clinging to the undersides of clouds.
The maples open overhead in tiers;
some fall behind to blaze a homeward path
of web-toed footprints. In what will be the first
of a hundred such befuddlements, you may
mistake the haze of sunset for a cloud
of leaf-smoke; or hanging brilliance for a fire
that's touched no leaf as yet.
                              Once in,
you're out again; the pavilion's doors have been
slid right off their grooves, and now the "walls"

are the garden's farther border, all of trees.
Awash in a mottled splash of maple color—
a backlit scarlet, a purple so dissonant
one shivers at the thought of it—the hard
and sturdy greenness of pine is a kind of anchor.

But looking across, your eyes may take in first—
under the great sasanqua tree, its white
blooms each set with a weighty orb of yellow
like a hard-boiled egg, halved on the horizontal—
a garden of sand, meant to make you thirst
for the color on the other side. And yet
even here sweeps the illusion of a sea:
around the rocks and thick tree trunk, a broom
of dried bamboo has combed into the dunes
fine, measured waves.   If you accept
a pair of rubber thongs from the attendant,
you can wade out past the azaleas that blaze
still in the wakened memory of those
visitors who return at every season;
if you are not yet one of us, imagine
how in May the blossoms, clipped down to just two
clusters or three on any bush, were tucked
neatly in leafy green as if behind
a young girl's ear. Time is safely kept here.
You can almost see it spinning in a wheel—
yet slowly, like those two birds overhead
swaying as if suspended in a mobile;

hung by the very hand, it seems, that frees
(even now, in autumn) two white butterflies
to spiral up in tandem, lift like kites
tethered to earth by strings too thin to see.

Ishikawa Jōzan had had time
to do almost everything before he built
this monument to possibility:
an attendant to a Tokugawa shōgun,
his service forbidden on the battlefield,
he defied this edict and, though having killed
to contribute to the shōgun's victory,
was denied all honors. Thus he became a scholar
in the Chinese classics, and at Hiroshima
was tutor to a feudal lord until
his mother died, who from the first had urged
that he should prove his worthiness at war.

Leaving the home he'd kept with her, he came
here to erect Shisendō and design
this celebrated garden, an example
of the "literary style"—which simply means
it grows in patterns that he freely chose. Look
how the towering *susuki* grass (each one
a long white brush that paints its own reflection)
fringes the pond it peers into, the lashes
of an eye that never closes.
                              A splash of carp—

a gold flash in the eye; and the picture's snapped
by the fear that one can never have it whole.
These maple tones (one autumn's variation
on a theme that's never played but in the thicket
of embellishment) you'll have to memorize
and superimpose upon next summer's green.
For now, attend the hollow bamboo rod—
shishiodōshi, so it's called, a word
mimicking how by a trickling waterfall
it's fed until it fills, and spills to knock
a metronomic *thonk* against a rock—
which, if it no longer frightens off
wild boars, as it was meant to, marks the time
precisely as it was, yet moves it on.

And so one still sees Ishikawa Jōzan
(as daylight fades again) climb to the turret
where every night for thirty quiet years,
the last of nearly ninety, he would watch
like a lighthouse-keeper, from a moon-shaped window,
for the moon's ship to come in.
                                                      Before it does,
you should make your way back past the spare azaleas,
back to the pavilion's darkest room
where (everything reminds of something else,
but nothing of what is not already here)
presides a glowing ring: the constellation
of the thirty-six ancient Chinese hermit-poets,

nine paintings to a wall, along the ceiling.
Most of them hatted, wispily bearded, old,
they sit patiently in brilliant folds of cloth
cut from the long bolt of time. Above their heads
fall poems in a few scrawled, simple lines.

He must have memorized them. But for us
it's enough to know each letter's packed with secrets,
like the *shi* of Shisendō, or "poetry":
composed of two linked characters— a "tongue"
jangling like the clapper on the bell
of "temple"—it rings but half a change
on the word for "word" itself: "tongue" joined to "leaf."
No accident perhaps, then, that the words
drifting above the poets' heads may call
up silently the leaves that you see falling
still through the pavilion's doorway.
                                        The light
is growing heavy, and unlike our host
who might see it all in night's continuum,
it's time for us to go—at least for now;
having come full-circle to the outer gate,
not certain where you are, a fallen star-
shaped maple leaf leads one step down
into Kyoto, where you'll wake tomorrow.

Mary Jo Salter was born in Grand Rapids, Michigan, and educated at Radcliffe College and Cambridge University. Her poems have appeared in a number of magazines and literary periodicals—among them *The Atlantic Monthly*, *The Kenyon Review*, *The Nation*, *The New Republic*, *The New Yorker*, and *Poetry*. She has been the recipient of an Academy of American Poets Prize, the Lloyd McKim Garrison Prize, and a National Endowment for the Arts Fellowship as well as co-winner of the annual "Discovery"/*The Nation* award and poet-in-residence at the Robert Frost Place in Franconia, New Hampshire. She is currently a lecturer in English literature at Mount Holyoke College.

A NOTE ON THE TYPE

The text of this book was set on the Monotype in Dante, a typeface designed by Dr. Giovanni Mardersteig for use at his famous press, Officina Bodoni, in Verona. Its first use was in an edition of Boccaccio's *Trattatello in laude di Dante* that appeared in 1954. In character the design of Dante is close to that of the Aldine old faces.

Composed by Heritage Printers, Inc.,
Charlotte, North Carolina.

Printed and bound by Halliday Lithographers,
Hanover, Massachusetts.

Typography and binding design by
Virginia Tan.